My St W... Y0-BEA-659

Consultants

Ashley Bishop, Ed.D.

Sue Bishop, M.E.D.

Publishing Credits

Dona Herweck Rice, *Editor-in-Chief*

Robin Erickson, *Production Director*

Lee Aucoin, *Creative Director*

Sharon Coan, *Project Manager*

Jamey Acosta, *Editor*

Rachelle Cracchiolo, M.A.Ed., *Publisher*

Image Credits

cover Eileen/BigStockPhoto; p.2 Mircea BEZERGHEANU/Shutterstock; p.3 fotohunter/Shutterstock; p.4 JazzIRT/iStockphoto; p.5 Elena Itsenko/Shutterstock; p.6 Eileen/BigStockPhoto; p.7 Gerville/iStockphoto; p.8 Dieter Spears/iStockphoto; p.9 photoflorenzo/Shutterstock; p.10 Ricardomss/BigStockPhoto; back cover Mircea BEZERGHEANU/Shutterstock

Teacher Created Materials

5301 Oceanus Drive
Huntington Beach, CA 92649-1030
http://www.tcmpub.com
ISBN 978-1-4333-3985-1
© 2012 Teacher Created Materials, Inc.

Look at the starfish.

Where is the starfish?

Look at the stapler.

Where is the stapler?

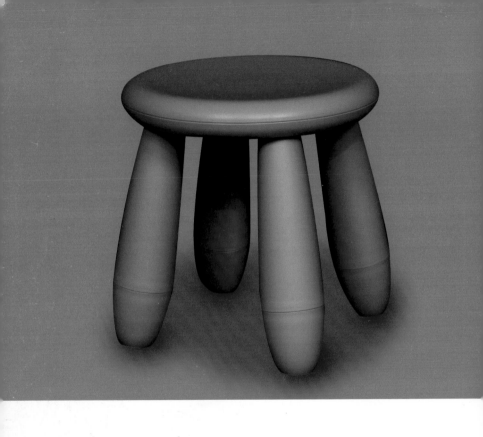

Look at the stool.

Where is the stool?

Look at the stoplight.

Where is the **st**oplight?

Look at the stairs.

Glossary

stairs

stapler

starfish

stool

stoplight

Sight Words

Look   at   the   Where   is

Activities

- Read the book aloud to your child, pointing to the *st* words. Help your child describe where the *st* objects are found.

- Draw a stoplight with your child. Have him or her add the words *stop*, *slow*, and *go* to the lights. Discuss street safety with your child.

- Check out a library book of ocean creatures. Learn about starfish, sea urchins, and sand dollars, together.

- Take the stairs instead of the elevator next time you get a chance.

- Imagine that you climb some stairs to a magical door. Share what you hope to find behind the door. Listen respectfully to each person's wishes.

- Help your child think of a personally valuable word to represent the letters *st*, such as *star*.